U.S. Environmental Protection Agency
U.S. Department of the Interior
Offices of Inspector General

Tribal Successes:

Protecting the Environment
and Natural Resources

May 2007

Credits

Special thanks to the following individuals for photos used in this report:

John S. Banks, Director, Dept. of Natural Resources, Penobscot Indian Nation
Nolan Colegrove, Forest Manager, Hoopa Valley Tribe
Ken Jock, Director, Environmental Division, Saint Regis Mohawk Tribe
Nancy John, Director, Environmental Programs, Cherokee Nation
Tim Keesey, Environmental Manager, Susanville Indian Rancheria
Charles Lujan, Director, Office of Environmental Affairs, Ohkay Owingeh
Dave Morgan, La Calandria Associates, Inc.
Staff, Offices of Inspector General for DOI and EPA

It is with great pleasure that we present *Tribal Successes: Protecting the Environment and Natural Resources*. Numerous Tribes use innovative practices to protect natural resources and the environment. This report showcases only a small sample of Tribal communities that demonstrate success in achieving natural resource and environmental goals. The overall intent of this report is to highlight examples of successful Tribal practices that will inspire and be useful to others in successfully implementing their own natural resource and environmental programs.

We extend our sincere thanks to all who provided feedback and suggestions. Your assistance greatly contributed to the design and completion of this report. We especially thank members of the Tribes highlighted in this report for their participation and interest. Their commitment to sharing successful Tribal programs and practices made this report possible.

This unique report is the culmination of a collaborative effort by the Offices of Inspector General for the U.S. Environmental Protection Agency and the U.S. Department of the Interior. It was prepared to promote Tribal programmatic capability and capacity. This report provides a forum to share the diversity of Tribal practices and to create models for success. We encourage government agencies and other stakeholders to use the report to enhance relationships and partnerships with Tribes.

Earl E. Devaney
Inspector General
U.S. Department of the Interior

Bill A. Roderick
Acting Inspector General
U.S. Environmental Protection Agency

Executive Summary

Tribal Successes: Protecting the Environment and Natural Resources

PURPOSE OF REPORT

This report was prepared to highlight the diversity of innovative Tribal practices that will serve as models of success to other Tribes in implementing natural resource and environmental programs. We also encourage U.S. Environmental Protection Agency and U.S. Department of the Interior officials and other stakeholders involved in promoting Tribal programmatic capability and capacity to use the report to enhance partnerships with Tribes.

INNOVATIVE PRACTICES

Successful implementation of environmental and natural resource projects directly results from innovative practices that overcome barriers. Some common barriers that affect Tribes include:

- Resource Limitations.
- Administrative and Managerial Requirements.
- Legal and Regulatory Issues.
- Communication and Relationships.

Some of the barriers affecting Tribal implementation of natural resource and environmental programs result from difficulties in working with federal entities. These difficulties often stem from differences in resource needs and availability, rules, operating procedures, goals, priorities, and culture.

Tribes have overcome barriers, such as those outlined above, through innovative practices, which are key variables for Tribes in maximizing the effectiveness of their programs. The innovative practices presented in this report are based on observations and examples provided by the 14 Tribes represented. Some of these practices include:

- Collaboration and Partnerships. Many of the successful Tribal projects resulted from efforts to foster good communication and positive relationships.
- Education and Outreach. Tribes value community input and understand that the success of many projects depends on community support. Natural resource and environmental projects are more effective if the community participates.
- Expanding Resources. Based on size, capacity, and structure, each of the Tribes represented has its own processes for securing resources to ensure sustainability in natural resource and environmental programs. In many cases, Tribes use available resources to market unique products. Some Tribes use an overall interest in Tribal culture and local attractions to promote tourism.

Table of Contents

THE 14 PARTICIPATING TRIBES

APPENDICES

Introduction

PURPOSE

The purpose of this collaborative effort is to highlight Tribes' successful management of environmental and natural resource programs. The effort was jointly conducted by the Offices of Inspector General for the U.S. Environmental Protection Agency (EPA) and the U.S. Department of the Interior (DOI).

Annette Islands Reserve

BACKGROUND

There are more than 560 federally recognized Tribes in the United States. Currently, these Tribes hold more than 50 million acres of land, or approximately 2 percent of the United States. Some Tribes hold as little as a few acres, and many Tribes hold no land at all. For example, in 1971, land title for Alaska Tribes was conveyed to Alaska Native Corporations, with the exception of the Annette Islands Reserve in southeast Alaska.

Each Tribe is an individual, sovereign government and is unique in structure and culture. Tribes operate their programs in a variety of ways. Common differences among Tribal operating methods include varying goals and objectives, administrative systems, funding

resources, and the capacity to implement projects.

Natural resources play a vital role in Tribal economies, which rely on land use, such as forestry and agriculture. Tribal communities also rely on the land for subsistence activities, such as hunting and fishing.

Land has always had great spiritual and cultural significance to the Tribes. To preserve the land, Tribes are committed to implementing environmental and natural resource programs. These programs include developing Tribal environmental regulations; managing solid and hazardous waste; and addressing issues of safe drinking water, sanitation, subsistence hunting and fishing, and cultural heritage preservation.

EPA supports Tribal environmental capacity building through its General Assistance Program, which provides opportunities for Tribes to develop core environmental programs. EPA's fiscal year 2006 goal was to provide funding and technical assistance for about 90 percent of federally recognized Tribal governments and intertribal consortia. DOI provides funding to promote self-governance and economic stability and works through its eight bureaus and offices to facilitate the growth and success of Tribal projects and programs.

Horses on Tribal Lands

Successful implementation of environmental and natural resource programs and projects is the direct outcome of innovative practices employed by the Tribes to overcome barriers. Many of the barriers affecting Tribal implementation of natural resource and environmental programs result from difficulties in working with federal entities, which may have differing rules, operating procedures, priorities, and resource limitations.

BARRIERS

The Tribes represented in this report provide numerous examples of successful implementation of environmental and natural resource projects and programs. Successful implementation is a continual challenge, however, and each Tribe faces numerous barriers. Some common barriers that affect Tribes include:

- ◆ Resource Limitations.
- ◆ Administrative and Managerial Requirements.
- ◆ Legal and Regulatory Issues.
- ◆ Communication and Relationships.

Resource Limitations. Tribes are continually looking for funds to initiate and successfully implement programs. Unfortunately, initiation of a program does not necessarily mean that it will be implemented. For example, Tribes that have difficulty in generating their own funding may face problems with continuing program operations. In addition, several Tribes informed us that federal assistance for operation and maintenance of programs is inadequate to meet program needs. As a result, some Tribes are forced to discontinue program participation when funding resources are exhausted.

Lack of funding also limits the Tribes' ability to attract and retain expert staff. Tribal staff turnover, however, is only one component of this

barrier. The represented Tribes explained that turnover of federal project officers is also a major issue. Replacement of project officers results in serious communication problems, such as the loss of project continuity and established relationships.

Administrative and Managerial Requirements. Tribes face the challenge of complying with changing federal rules and regulations, which vary among federal agencies. The procedures and processes a Tribe uses to meet one agency's requirements may not be applicable when dealing with another agency. In some cases, incompatibilities also exist among Tribal and federal administrative systems.

Inefficiencies occur when Tribes are required to follow different procedures from one federal agency to another. These inefficiencies can lead to additional Tribal resource needs. In some cases, differences in procedures are drastic enough to discourage Tribes from pursuing federal assistance.

Legal and Regulatory Issues. Federal program regulations limit the use of funds to particular activities or functions. Such limitations may affect the Tribes' ability to manage their programs, and in some cases, Tribes have refused funding because of use

Indian Island, Eureka, CA

Boats Used for Subsistence Fishing

limitations. In other cases, authority may overlap among multiple federal agencies, causing confusion because of differing regulatory language.

Tribal land bases also vary considerably. Some Tribes have rights to an undivided land base while other Tribes have no land base at all. Most Tribes reside in areas that are divided into sections of Tribal and non-Tribal land. As a result, Tribes cannot enforce their regulations on non-Tribal land within Tribal boundaries.

Communication and Relationships. A lack of understanding about Tribal cultures among non-Tribal entities is another barrier. Non-Tribal officials do not always consider unique Tribal cultures when working with Tribes. Some Tribes believe the federal officials they work with do not adequately understand Tribal sovereignty or the federal trust responsibility. Furthermore, federal agencies do not always coordinate with each other when they share program oversight, resulting in inconsistent information being provided to Tribes.

INNOVATIVE PRACTICES

Tribes have overcome barriers, such as those outlined previously, through innovative practices. Innovation is a key variable for Tribes to maximize the effectiveness of their programs. Some of the practices used by the represented Tribes include:

- ♦ Collaboration and Partnerships.
- ♦ Education and Outreach.
- ♦ Expanding Resources.

Collaboration and Partnerships. Many successful Tribal projects result from efforts to foster good communication and positive relationships. Represented Tribes expressed a strong desire to collaborate with a diverse group of partners, such as the local community, non-profits, private industry, other Tribes, and state and federal agencies. These Tribes understand that environmental and natural resource issues are not limited by jurisdictional boundaries and that partnerships are based on common objectives, creating an increase in resources, knowledge, and experience. The end result is broadened program success.

Wolf River, WI

The involvement of non-Tribal entities can enhance the success of natural resource or environmental projects. Good communication and credibility established through proven Tribal success can influence non-Tribal entities.

Education and Outreach. Tribes value Tribal community input and understand that the success of many projects depends on community support. Natural resource and environmental projects are more effective if the community participates. One Tribe informed us that Tribal community input is often the most valuable measure of project success.

The Tribes represented use numerous approaches to educate surrounding communities about environmental and natural resource issues. Outreach activities range from formal community meetings to classroom visits and fieldtrips. Some Tribes also use media, such as pamphlets, cartoons, and computer learning aids, to enhance outreach.

In some cases, education and outreach extend beyond surrounding communities. Tribal project and program successes influence others to institute similar approaches. By creating and

carrying out innovative practices, Tribes demonstrate the possibility of accomplishing planned natural resource and environmental goals. These positive results motivate other Tribes and communities to adapt proven innovative practices to fit their own natural resource and environmental needs, thereby demonstrating that successes are transferable beyond the boundaries of a single Tribe.

Expanding Resources. Based on the size, capacity, and structure of the Tribe, each of the Tribes represented has its own processes for securing resources to sustain natural resource and environmental programs. In many cases, Tribes use available resources to market unique products. Some Tribes build on an overall interest in Tribal culture to attract tourism and market their accomplishments.

To overcome funding limitations, several Tribes diversify revenue sources for their programs. For example, some Tribes obtain and combine funding from multiple agencies to implement a single natural resource or environmental program. Other Tribes establish relationships and partnerships to create or obtain support from non-profit organizations. Such relationships expand outreach and support and are an effective approach to raising funds for programs.

Tribes also expand available resources by increasing efficiency. One way to increase efficiency is through diversifying employee skills. Expanded skills allow individual employees to accomplish tasks that would otherwise require additional personnel.

The Tribes noted in the illustration on page 5 and on the map on pages 6-7 demonstrate the successes achieved through the use of collaboration and partnerships, education and outreach, and expanding resources to resolve environmental and natural resource challenges.

Innovative Recycling Container

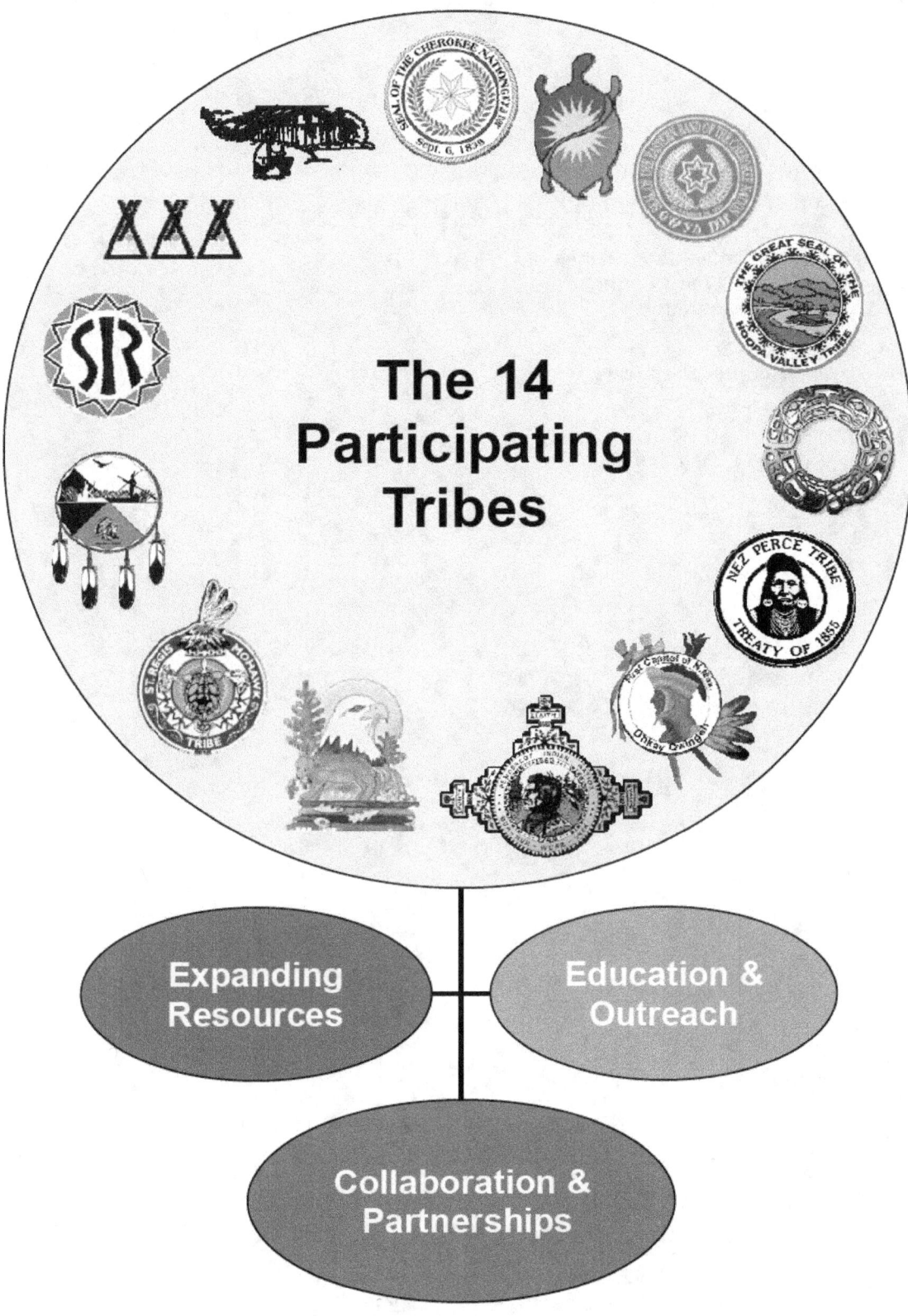

The 14 Participating Tribes

Expanding Resources

Education & Outreach

Collaboration & Partnerships

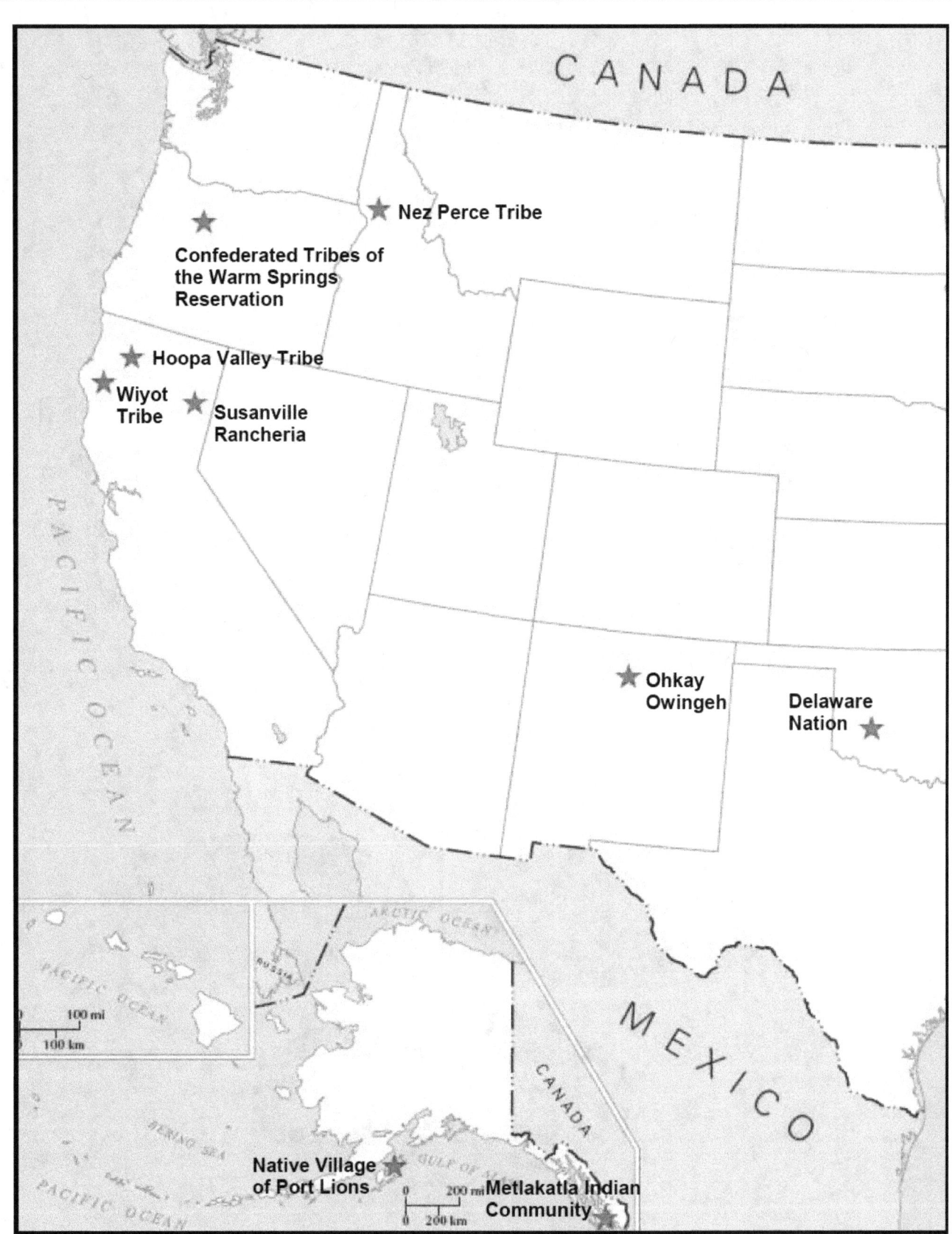

Cherokee Nation

With the discovery of gold in Georgia in the 1830s, settlers began to covet the Cherokee homelands. A period of Indian Removals made way for more settlement. In 1838, thousands of Cherokee men, women, and children were rounded up and marched 1,000 miles to Indian Territory, known today as the State of Oklahoma. That journey is remembered as the "Trail of Tears." A spirit of survival and perseverance carried the Cherokee to Indian Territory in 1838, and leads the Cherokee today.

Consisting of 262,316 citizens, the Cherokee Nation is the one of the largest Tribes in the United States. Of these citizens, 133,247 live within the Nation's jurisdiction, which encompasses eight counties and portions of six other counties in northeastern Oklahoma – an area of about 700 square miles.

The Cherokee Nation administers environmental programs through the executive branch of its government. Two primary administrators are the Environmental Protection Commission and the Department of Natural Resources.

The Commission oversees environmental functions related to natural resource projects, such as reviewing proposed legislation, approving or disapproving legislation, promulgating regulations, exercising penalty and enforcement authority, and overseeing compliance with the National Environmental Policy Act. The Department of Natural Resources oversees programs such as forestry, land, and invasive species management, and is currently developing an Integrated Resources Management Plan. The purpose of the Plan is to facilitate planning and execution that merge environmental and natural resource data, processes, and actions.

Methamphetamine Lab Assessments

The Cherokee Nation developed a methamphetamine (meth) lab assessment initiative because of concerns about the nationwide meth use epidemic. The Nation gained the knowledge and expertise necessary to control the environmental and health risks associated with meth labs and assess lab sites to ensure harmful chemicals are not still present.

The level of contamination found at a meth lab site depends on a number of factors, including the method used to produce meth, cooking duration, location, and ventilation. Of particular concern is the threat of residual contamination, which can result from spills; leakage; absorption by porous materials; and hazardous leftover materials, such as phosphene gas "death bags," metals, and salts. Often, health problems (headaches, dizziness, and skin disorders) can occur when sites are reoccupied. Children are at a higher risk because their immune systems are

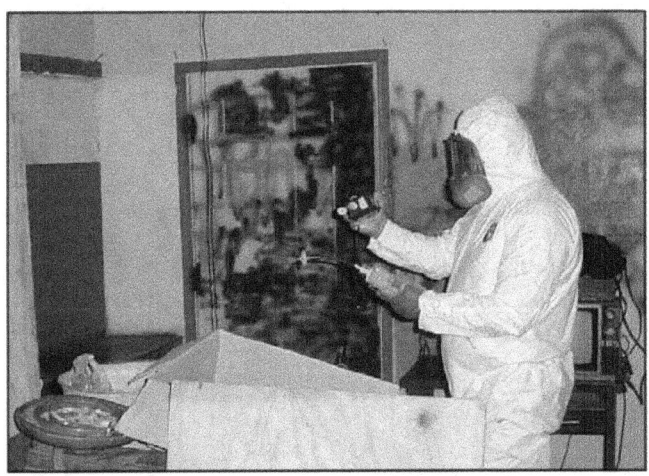

Meth Lab Assessment

not as highly developed as those of adults. Children also crawl and play on the floor, where contaminants are likely to exist.

In addition to the assessments, the initiative has increased awareness throughout the Cherokee Nation and surrounding communities about the health and environmental risks associated with

Meth Lab Assessments & Air Monitoring

meth production. The Nation conducts training about the hazards of meth lab assessments and plans to expand the training to Tribal organizations nationwide.

Community Air Monitoring Station

data collected by the Nation is broadly available to outside entities. Data from each station is automatically downloaded to a public site (the EPA AIRNow website) every hour, thereby benefiting not only the Nation, but also local communities and the state.

The Cherokee Nation also participates in several national air monitoring programs, including Interagency Monitoring of Protected Visual Environments Regional Haze, CastNet Rural Ozone Monitoring, Mercury Deposition Network, National Trends Network, National Core Network Monitoring Programs, and Community Air Toxics.

Air Monitoring Activities

According to Cherokee Nation officials, the Nation's air monitoring network—six continuous monitoring shelters scattered throughout the Nation's land base—is the largest Tribal air monitoring network in the United States. In fact, the Nation's network is larger than networks in several states. To ensure consistency in operations and maintenance, the Nation generally uses standard equipment at each site. Each air monitoring station routinely collects data on "criteria pollutants" (carbon monoxide, sulfur oxide, nitrogen oxide, ozone, and particulate matter).

The Nation's air monitoring network is used for numerous special studies. The air monitoring

> **"Breaking the cycle of drug addiction requires strong support for prevention, enforcement, treatment, and environmental health.
> We hope to contribute to this through our anti-meth coalition."**
>
> —— Chad Smith
> **Cherokee Nation Principal Chief**

Contact: Nancy John, Director, Cherokee Nation Environmental Programs, 918-453-5000 or njohn@cherokee.org

Delaware Nation

The Delaware, once a confederacy, occupied the entire basin of the Delaware River in eastern Pennsylvania and southwest New York, together with most of New Jersey and Delaware. The Delaware called themselves Lenape, meaning "the people," while settlers knew them as the Delaware from the name of their principal river. Gradually, the Delaware were relocated West and split into two groups just before the Civil War. One group, the Delaware Tribe, moved through Kansas and then into Indian Territory in Oklahoma, where the Tribe still lives.

The second group, which would eventually become the Delaware Nation, also moved to Oklahoma and reorganized under the Oklahoma Indian Welfare Act of 1936. In April 1973, this group passed a Tribal Constitution changing its name to the Delaware Nation of Western Oklahoma. In 1984, the group moved into new offices located about 2 miles north of Anadarko, Oklahoma. In November 1999, the group changed its name to the Delaware Nation, with a membership of 1,298.

Environmental problems faced by the Delaware Nation include air quality issues (high ozone levels and asthma), hazardous waste, pesticides, and open dump sites. To address these problems, the Delaware Nation initiated an environmental program in October 1997. The Nation's environmental office is staffed by eight employees.

The Delaware Nation is working towards an overall goal to establish internal capacity and capability to conserve, preserve, and protect the environment. To achieve this goal, the Nation provides training for the environmental staff and uses up-to-date technology and processes to identify and develop strategies to manage problem areas.

Air Monitoring Activities

Air quality issues are important to the Delaware Nation because of potential pollutants from

Air Monitoring Station

nearby power plants, interstate highways, and diesel-powered drilling by oil companies. Concerned about the effect of poor air quality on human health and the environment and the lack of overall air monitoring data for southwest Oklahoma, the Nation implemented a process to evaluate air quality.

The Nation obtained assistance to establish an air monitoring station and began monitoring activities in November 2002. Passive ozone testing in 2003 and 2004 revealed high ozone levels. To obtain a more complete picture of air quality, the Nation is working to expand monitoring activities to include assessments of nitrogen oxide and particulate matter. Since air pollution is not confined to

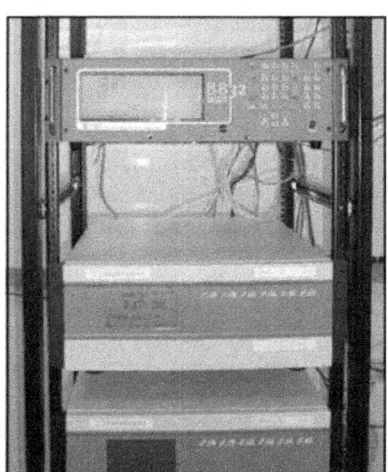
Air Monitoring Equipment

its boundaries, the Nation sees its air monitoring activities as important practices for the entire surrounding community.

Recycling

In spite of several challenges, the Delaware Nation successfully implemented a rural recycling program in cooperation with nearby Tribes and the City of Anadarko. A collection facility is located on the reservation, but services are offered throughout the local community. The Nation provides recycling services at community events, and City officials recently asked the Nation to install a large recycling station at City Hall. Although the program is currently limited to recycling aluminum and paper products, participation in the program has grown to the point that the Nation plans to expand into recycling plastics and appliances.

One of the biggest challenges faced by the Nation was a lack of interest by community residents, who were accustomed to disposing of waste through other means, such as burning. The Nation is successfully meeting this challenge through an outreach program to educate residents about the benefits of proper disposal. Actions taken by the Nation include visiting schools and working with the community health board to ensure residents are better informed. The Nation's outreach has increased participation in the recycling program, and the program continues to grow. To sustain and expand the program, the Nation charges each

Bales of Shredded Paper for Recycling

user $20 per month to cover waste pick-up and recycling services.

The volume of material recycled or eliminated from the waste stream through the Delaware Nation's program averages 200 tons per year. In addition, the success of the recycling program has resulted in the creation of four jobs. The Nation targets motivated employees to work in the program and provides adequate training. Sustainability is an important issue to the Nation and has been a primary factor in the growth and success of the recycling program.

> **"Environmental Programs will protect, enhance, promote, preserve and regulate our native lands, water and air."**
>
> —— **Mission Statement, Delaware Nation Environmental Programs**

Community Recycling Bin

Contact: Nikki Owings-Crumm, Acting Director, Delaware Nation Environmental Program, 405-247-2448 ext 137 or nyocrumm@delawarenation.com

Eastern Band of Cherokee

In 1838, thousands of Cherokee were forcibly removed from their land in North Carolina and taken to Oklahoma on the "Trail of Tears." The Cherokee in western North Carolina today are descendents of those who were able to hold on to land they owned; those who hid in the hills, defying removal; and those who returned, many on foot. Today, the Band is composed of about 12,000 members.

The Band's land encompasses over 56,000 contiguous acres adjacent to the Great Smoky Mountains National Park in North Carolina. Natural resources and the environment have served as touchstones for Tribal traditions and as sources of income for decades. Tourism is important to the Band's economy, and cold-water trout streams are primary local attractions.

The Eastern Band of Cherokee strives to conserve local natural resources for continued use and enjoyment by successive generations. The Band's Office of Environment and Natural Resources started operation in October 1992 and increased its activity in 2000, when the Band used grant funds to hire people with the expertise to successfully apply for additional grants. Seventy percent of funding for the Office is obtained through grants, and 30 percent is provided by the Band.

The Band is working to address the challenge of hiring and retaining qualified people, a challenge that is made more difficult by the fact that employees wear "multiple hats". Loss of an employee is therefore a severe setback because more than one function has to be replaced. The Band is trying to maintain its knowledge base by certifying people and keeping them current through training programs like those offered by the United South and Eastern Tribes.

Conversion of Open Dump and Solid Waste Recycling

After careful planning, the Eastern Band of Cherokee covered a large open dump for use as a staging area for water, sewer, sanitation, construction, and other Tribal projects.

Crusher at Converted Open Dump

The Band uses the site to recycle soil, concrete, and asphalt from outside contractors. Soil is sifted and refined through a shaker owned by the Band, and waste rock is crushed to gravel with a crusher donated by the U.S. Army in 2003. Recycled soil and rock are used on Tribal and U.S. Forest Service roads, and private citizens purchase material from the Band to use on driveways and around barns. The Band began turning a profit on the crusher in 2006 and hopes to earn enough to buy a bigger crusher. The site also serves as a training ground for the Band's young people, who can learn to operate heavy machinery and be educated in other aspects of construction. After training, these young people possess the technical skills and experience to be marketable in a variety of trades.

Recycling Center

Managing Solid Waste & Restoring Habitat

The former dump houses the Band's recycling center. Begun in 1989, the Band's Recycling Department promotes reducing, recycling, and reusing solid waste and diverting waste like aluminum cans and paper products from landfills. A goal is to reduce solid waste disposal costs on Tribal lands to the greatest extent possible. About 13,000 local residents and 30 businesses currently participate in the program. In 2006, the recycling program diverted about 640,000 pounds of solid waste (aluminum, glass, plastic, paper and cardboard), 200 used car batteries, and 1,700 gallons of used motor oil from landfills.

The Band's Sanitation Department runs a composting program, with educational seminars attended by people from as far away as Ohio, and sells its own compost locally. The Band

Erosion Control

created a nationally used manual *Composting Made Simple*, distributed by EPA. The Band's Sanitation Department was a 1992 National Finalist in Harvard University's Award for Stewardship and Sanitation and won an EPA Award for Outstanding Stewardship and Environmentalism in 2000.

Stream Restoration and Water Quality

The Band used $60,000 of its own money, low-cost and volunteer labor, logs from trees removed from a Tribal school construction site, and donated rock to control stream bank erosion in a high-traffic, urban recreation area. The Band also used rock to build ledges, shoals, and water features within the stream to enhance trout habitat. The project was large and high profile. It was certified by the Bureau of Indian Affairs as a low impact development and will be

featured in the North American Green's *Erosion Discussion* newsletter as one of the most diverse projects in the nation in terms of planning.

By using its own resources, the Band completed the project at one-fourth to one-third of the cost of using outside contractors. The project is closely connected to the Band's water quality monitoring efforts. The Band is one of the few Tribes east of the Mississippi that collects as well as evaluates water quality data.

Fish Hatchery

Stream restoration and good water quality support the Band's fish hatchery program, which stocks recreational and commercial ponds with about 360,000 fish each year. Locally, both rivers and ponds are used for recreational fishing. The Band charges $150 for a seasonal fishing permit. The Band believes that stocking recreational and commercial ponds and streams with farmed trout takes pressure off wild populations and is collaborating with the U.S. Fish and Wildlife Service to stock non-game fish to maintain water wildlife diversity.

> **"As we continue our journey, we forge the paths for those with a clearer vision for our future."**
>
> ——**Eastern Band of the Cherokee Nation 2004 Annual Report**

Contact: Edward Huskey, Deputy Operating Officer, Eastern Band of Cherokee, 828-497-1805 or ehuskey@nc-cherokee.com

Hoopa Valley Tribe

Members of the Hoopa Valley Tribe are known as Hupa. They live in and around the town of Hoopa in northern California and total 1,800 of the town's population of 2,500. Of the 92,500 acres comprising the Tribe's reservation, 88,000 are considered to be commercial forest land.

Today, the Hupa are working to restore the natural resources that were damaged by federal land and water development and management. From the 1950s to the late 1980s, the Bureau of Indian Affairs managed the Tribe's forests, focusing primarily on maximizing revenue. The result was the clear cutting of 33,000 acres to annually produce about 60 million board feet of timber. The clear cuts re-moved plants and animals and degraded water quality and fish habitat.

Prior Clear-Cut Forest Practices

Water development by the Bureau of Reclamation also degraded water quality and fisheries. The Hupa live within the Klamath River watershed, and the Trinity River, a Klamath tributary, bisects the reservation. In 1963, the Trinity River was dammed to divert up to 90 percent of its water. This diversion, combined with competing demands for water by farmers, hydropower users, and fishermen, has severely strained the entire Klamath River ecosystem.

In 2002, low flows in the Trinity resulted in higher water temperatures, overcrowding, and the spread of bacteria, all of which killed an estimated 60,000 salmon during a 2-week period. Fish tags revealed that two-thirds of the fish were from the Trinity River.

Sustainable Forest Management

A sustainable forest is critical, as timber is the source of about 95 percent of the Tribe's annual discretionary revenue. The Tribe took over management of its Forestry Program in 1989 and by 1994 had adopted a Forest Management Plan laying out a Tribal vision to balance economic return with forest resource protection 120 years into the future. The Tribe reduced the annual allowable cut to about 10 million board feet; began restoring clear-cut lands through tree regeneration; classified significant acreage as no-cut; and controlled erosion, which also helped reduce stream sediment and protect fish habitat.

FMP Landbase
Restrictions
NO CUT
INTENSIVE
PARTIAL CUT
URBAN
FEE/ALLOT

Hoopa Valley Reservation

An innovative practice solved the problem of black bears stripping the bark from young Douglas fir trees to feed on the sweet layer of wood underneath, thereby killing the trees. The Tribe rejected practices used by other timber companies, ranging from killing to feeding the bears, in favor of DNA testing to identify problem bears. After a 2-year study, the Tribe can identify these bears by the condition of their teeth and remove the bears to other locations. The Tribe also changed its forestry practices to leave a greater number of older trees intact, making them less attractive to bears.

Sustainable Forestry & Water Protection

In 1999, Tribal forestry practices were certified as meeting professional forest sustainability standards developed by the Forest Stewardship Council,[1] a global network located in more than 40 countries.

Sustainable Forestry

The Tribe viewed certification as a way to develop a market premium for Tribal wood products and provide an outside assessment of forest management to Tribal members. The Council ensures ongoing compliance through annual audits, which the Tribe has consistently passed.

By including its Cultural Committee in forest management decisions, the Tribe protects cultural resources that were not protected under previous practices. For example, basket-making materials are now protected by a cultural burning program to regenerate cultural plants, by a prohibition on herbicides on the reservation, and by an agreement with the U.S. Forest Service to ban herbicides on adjoining National Forest land. Every year, the Tribe allocates funding to manually treat competing vegetation throughout its forest. While costly, this practice protects resources, human health, and fish habitat.

Water Quality Protection

The Hupa were the first California Tribe to develop water quality standards approved by EPA. With continuous data recorders measuring up to 20 parameters, the Tribe collects baseline data and monitors the presence of macro-invertebrates to evaluate stream health over time. It also regularly tests water quality and uses the results to strengthen

Klamath River Fish Kill in 2002

water quality standards and better manage water resources. For example, in response to the 2002 fish kill, the Tribe developed standards, now awaiting EPA approval, for the presence of bacteria in reservation waters to help prevent future catastrophic fish kills. The Tribe is also working with the courts and federal agencies to restore higher flows to the Trinity River.

The Bureau of Reclamation acceded to the Tribe's request to release additional water into the Trinity River in late August and early September for the annual Hoopa Boat Dance Ceremonies, which use river water for sweat houses and cultural bathing. Because of the work of the Hoopa Valley and other Tribes, California's North Coast Water Quality Control Plan now includes provisions for the cultural use of water.

> **"To us, the river is a way of life.**
> **We live, work and play**
> **in that water.**
> **It's something**
> **we've always had,**
> **and something we plan**
> **to always have in the future."**
>
> —Joseph Jarnaghan,
> former Hoopa Valley Council Member

Contacts: Nolan Colegrove, Forest Manager, 530-625-4284 or nolanccsr@pcweb.net
Ken Norton, Director, Tribal EPA, 530-625-5515 or knorton@hoopa-nsn.gov
Hoopa Valley Tribe

---

[1] The Council accredits independent third-parties to certify that forest managers and product producers meet Council forest management standards. The Tribe was certified through the Rainbow Alliance's SmartWood program.

Metlakatla Indian Community

The Metlakatla Indian Community is located on the Annette Islands Reserve and encompasses 86,313 acres of land and 46,019 acres of water, for a total of 132,332 acres. Located in southeast Alaska, it is the only federal Indian reserve in the state. In 1940, the U.S. Army built an air base on 12,783 acres located 6 miles south of the town of Metlakatla. The base brought runways, taxi routes, hangars, storage tanks, facilities, housing, docks, a hospital, and infrastructure improvements to water, sewage, and communications.

At the end of World War II, the air base was vacated, and in 1948, the Federal Aviation Administration leased the base for use as the Ketchikan Airport. Control shifted to the U.S. Coast Guard in 1956, and by 1973 the airport had been moved to a new facility closer to Ketchikan. All remaining airport support activity ceased in 1977.

Subsequently, the timber and fishing industries supporting the Community were steadily declining. Increases in farmed salmon negatively affected the wild fish industry, and the fish cannery in Metlakatla closed. The 1999 closure of the Annette Hemlock Mill effectively stopped the timber harvest. To find jobs for its members, the Community decided to diversify its economy and improve the quality of life for all Community members, while remaining sensitive to its cultural and environmental values.

In 1996, the Community's Environmental Coordinator, working with a contractor, identified more than 80 sites associated with former federal facilities near Metlakatla. Of these sites, 72 had problems, including leaking drums, asbestos, lead, pesticides, polychlorinated biphenyls, chemical and oil spills, and leaking above and underground storage tanks.

Good planning and decisive action over the past few years have helped the Metlakatla Indian Community make significant progress in cleaning up the Annette Islands and diversifying its economy. The success of the cleanup was such that in 2000 the Community was designated as a Brownfields Showcase Community,[1] one of 28 Showcase Communities in the United States and one of only two Tribes to be so designated.

The cleanup used a Community workforce whenever possible, and several members earned Hazardous Waste Operations and Emergency Response certifications to form a skilled labor pool. Economic successes also include the Community's Purple Mountain Pure Water Bottling Plant, opened in 2003, and ongoing planning for a rock quarry that could produce an estimated 200 million tons of rock over a 40-year life, employ 60 Community members, and generate nearly $1 billion in revenues.

A Showcase Community

As a Showcase Community, the Community's goal is to promote self-governance and serve as a model for other Tribal communities experiencing similar environmental issues. Key to the success of the cleanup were Memorandums of Understanding with agencies that had contributed to the contamination. A Work Group composed of

Annette Island

---

[1] EPA initiated its Brownfields Program in 1995 to empower states and other entities to boost local economies by cleaning up brownfields, defined as properties whose reuse could be compromised by the presence of contaminants. There are an estimated 450,000 brownfields in the United States.

Collaboration & Economic Development

Abandoned Structure

members of the Community and staff from the Bureau of Indian Affairs, Federal Aviation Administration, U.S. Army Corps of Engineers, U.S. Coast Guard, National Weather Service, and Chevron Texaco Company has made notable progress. Accomplishments include dismantling and disposing of eight contaminated buildings and pads, removing 700 tons of scrap metal, draining and cleaning 10,000 feet of fuel line, removing 7,000 gallons of mixed fuel and water, demolishing and recycling 45 abandoned towers with lead-based paint, removing and recycling 800 abandoned drums, and disposing of 14 underground and one aboveground fuel storage tanks. Fuel-contaminated soil was creatively used to repave roads throughout the reservation.

The Community also took the lead on several projects administered by the Department of Defense, such as the Moss Point Garrison, where 42 collapsed buildings, a fuel tank, a septic tank, and several hundred cubic yards of contaminated soil were removed. At the White Alice Station, a former U.S. Air Force site, 137 abandoned transformers, two underground fuel storage tanks, one aboveground storage tank, and several thousand cubic yards of contaminated soil were removed.

A Diversified Economy

The Community's Purple Mountain Pure Water Bottling Plant takes advantage of the 180 inches of rain that falls each year on the Annette Islands. Water is taken from the town water system, whose source is a nearby lake, and filtered, de-chlorinated, and ozone purified. The plant is capable of processing 600 bottles per

hour and ships about 1,000 cases (480,000 bottles) per month. The goal is to sell bottled water to the lower 48 states.

Rock, another natural resource, is the basis for the Bald Ridge Aggregate Project, a proposed quarry that would create jobs by providing high-quality crushed rock to the Pacific Northwest through the Metlakatla Aggregate Construction Company. The Metlakatla Community has completed surface sampling and testing; exploratory drilling; and engineering, environmental, and marketing studies. It is now seeking contracts with the U.S. Army Corps of Engineers for sale of the rock.

Purple Mountain Pure Bottled Water

The Community has also submitted applications for certification as a small and disadvantaged business to the Department of Transportation and the Small Business Administration.

> **"Our main goal is making sure that the community and island will be self-sustaining.**
>
> **We have an abundance of resources and want to keep them."**
>
> —— Metlakatla Member

Contact: Jeff Benson, Environmental Coordinator, Metlakatla Indian Community, 907-886-4200 or micenviro@hotmail.com

17

Nez Perce Tribe

The Nez Perce, or Nimiipuu as they refer to themselves, originally occupied about 13 millions acres in what is now southeastern Washington, northeastern Oregon, and northern Idaho. The Treaty of 1855 resulted in the Tribe relinquishing 5.5 million acres to the U.S. government and an 1863 treaty further reduced the reservation to about 750,000 acres.

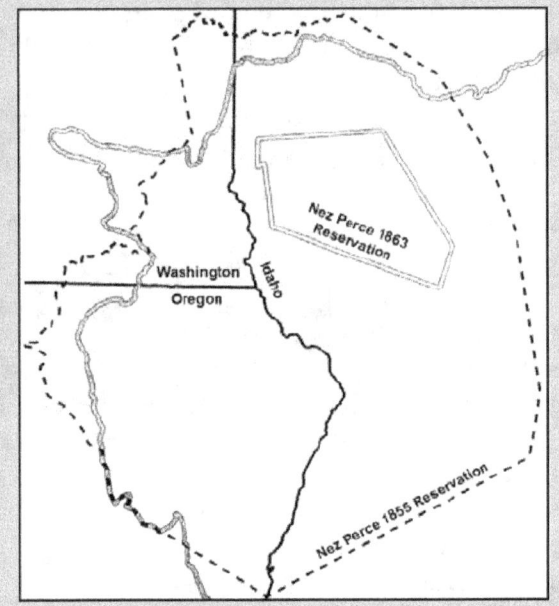

Passage of the Dawes Act in 1887 opened the reservation to homesteading, allowing non-Indians to buy reservation land and create a "checkerboard" pattern of land ownership. Today, the Nez Perce own only about 12 percent of the reservation, resulting in issues over jurisdiction. About 18,000 people live within reservation boundaries, including about 1,600 of the Tribe's 3,900 members.

The Tribe established a Natural Resources Department to provide for the Tribe's long-term cultural, social, political, and economic stability. The Department has divisions for cultural resources, environmental restoration and waste management, forestry, land services, water resources, and wildlife.

18

Monitoring Air Quality

Air quality is a concern for everyone who lives on the reservation because of three large lumber mills; woodstoves; residential, forestry and agricultural burning; and other sources. Several communities are located in the river valley which is prone to air inversions. The Tribe administers EPA's Federal Air Regulations for Reservations (FARR), which regulates air emissions within the boundaries of 39 reservations in Idaho, Oregon, and Washington. The Tribe has a full-time outreach person on staff and has held meetings with the community, city governments, and emergency service agencies.

In 1998, the Tribe received EPA funding to address air quality issues and now operates air equipment at three locations to monitor particulates and toxics, including metals, carbonyls and volatile organic compounds. The Tribe coordinates air quality management with the State of Idaho, which uses Tribal air quality data to help determine when to issue burn permits off-reservation. The State's Department of Environmental Quality posts State and Tribal monitoring data on its website.

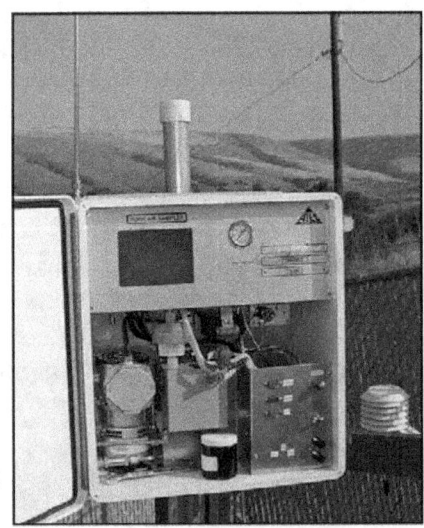

Air Monitoring Station

Since 2002, the Tribe has coordinated smoke management operations with other agencies through a four-party agreement with EPA and Idaho's Departments of Agriculture and Environmental Quality. The Tribe's program includes the FARR residential, agricultural and forestry burn-permitting process, which emphasizes cooperation and coordination with burners. The Tribe acts as EPA's representative on the reservation, but sends investigations to EPA for enforcement action. A database tracks burn permits and air quality, and an approved burn list is shared with the other agencies each day. The Tribe uses forecasting tools and the monitoring network to issue permits and burn bans.

Reintroducing Gray Wolves

The Tribe contracted with the U.S. Fish and Wildlife Service to lead gray wolf recovery efforts in Idaho. In 1999, Harvard University's Project on American Indian Economic Development recognized the Tribe and its contributions to the Wolf Recovery Program with an "Honoring Nations" award. The success of the Wolf Recovery Program represents a cultural triumph to the Nez Perce people, since their heritage includes a reverence for wildlife.

The Wolf Recovery Program was the first time the federal government contracted with a Native American Tribe to manage recovery of an endangered species. The goal of the U.S. Fish and Wildlife Service was to have 10 breeding pairs in each of the recovery areas (Idaho, Montana, and Wyoming) for 3 years. In the first 2 years of the Program (1995-97), the Tribe released 35 wolves into the Idaho wilderness. In 1998, through monitoring radio-collared wolves, the Tribe documented 10 breeding pairs, thereby meeting the recovery goal for Idaho. By 2005, the wolf population had grown to 512 individuals, with 36 breeding pairs producing 123 pups.

To overcome deep-rooted fear and misunderstanding of wolves, the Tribe conducted seminars to educate the public. It also partnered with the Wolf Education and Research Center to establish a visitor center on the reservation. The center increases public awareness by using four gray wolves to serve as ambassadors for the Program. Born in captivity, these wolves live in a 20-acre enclosure that is one of the largest of its kind in North America.

Gray Wolf at Wolf Education and Research Center

In addition to public education efforts, the Nez Perce Tribe developed ways to mitigate concerns of ranchers and the State of Idaho about wolf-livestock conflicts. To address these concerns, the Tribe compensates ranchers for losses through a fund established in conjunction with Defenders of Wildlife, a non-profit organization. The State of Idaho has established a compensation fund, and is working with the Tribe to manage wolf populations.

> **"The sanctuary on the Nez Perce Reservation will provide for our Tribal members an opportunity to experience a reunification of the cultural and spiritual bond. In turn it will allow the non Indian world to experience the same."**
>
> **—Levi Holt, former chair of the Nez Perce Fish and Wildlife Committee**

Contact: Aaron Miles Sr., Manager, Department of Natural Resources, Nez Perce Tribe, 208-843-7400 ext. 2380 or 2moon@nezperce.org

Ohkay Owingeh

Named for "the place of the strong people," the Ohkay Owingeh Tribe in New Mexico comprises about 2,400 people, of whom about 2,100 live on the Tribe's Pueblo. There are 450 homes on Tribally owned land, but close to 12,000 people live within Tribal boundaries, and 30,000 people live within a 10-mile radius. According to the Ohkay Owingeh, the Pueblo has been continuously occupied for over 700 years. The Rio Grande and the Rio Chama crisscross Tribal lands. All local drinking water is either well water or other groundwater outlets.

The Tribe began using its Tewa name "Ohkay Owingeh" in November 2005, after having gone by the Spanish name "San Juan Pueblo" since the days of Spanish rule in the late 16th century. Ohkay Owingeh is the name of the starting place of the August 10, 1680 Pueblo Revolt against Spanish rule, and the Eight Northern Indian Pueblos Council is headquartered on the Pueblo. Every July, a native crafts fair is held on the Eight Northern Pueblos grounds, attended by about 24,000.

The Ohkay Owingeh have few economic resources: the finance department is small; staff turnover is a problem; and funding is continually an issue. To overcome these barriers, Tribal officials continue to look for new opportunities to create funding and growth. For example, the Tribe rents out spaces in its RV park. Tsay, a Tribe-owned corporation, owns and operates the Ohkay Owingeh casino and hotel. The Tribe raises cattle and leases land for cattle grazing as well as a Tribally-owned radio/cell phone tower. The Tribe has also built community low-income housing on Pueblo lands and received the 2004 National Award for Smart Growth Achievement from the EPA.

Wetlands Restoration

The Ohkay Owingeh began restoring wetlands to reverse the adverse effects associated with a channel project on the Rio Grande conducted by the U.S. Army Corps of Engineers. In the 1950s,

Former Wetland

the Corps channeled, diked and ultimately straightened the Rio Grande to control flooding. The channel project, however, removed water from the

bosque,[1] and the native vegetation and wildlife associated with that environment disappeared. Straightening the river also affected humans because wetlands act as a secondary filtration system for water. Water eventually goes back into the ground and becomes part of the groundwater system. As all Tribal water came from wells or other groundwater outlets, the Tribe's water quality decreased with straightening of the river.

The Tribe is currently restoring 750 acres: some have already been restored; others are being restored, and still others are in the restoration planning proc-

Restored Wetland

ess. A contractor guides Tribal restoration efforts, with much of the work done by volunteers and students. The Tribe closely monitors restoration efforts because conditions on the Pueblo,

---

[1] Bosque is the name for areas of riparian forest found along the flood plains of stream and river banks in the southwestern United States.

Wetlands Restoration & Waste Management

especially in the bosque area, continue to change and evolve. Tribal officials estimate 1,500 to 2000 acres within the Pueblo could be restored as wetlands.

The Tribe is also working with outside communities to restore wetlands and improve overall water quality. Many of the Tribe's wetland restoration efforts are now being copied along other portions of the Rio Grande. Successful wetland restoration has resulted in revival of the beaver population. The Ohkay Owingeh consider beaver to be the Tribe's "natural volunteers," as beaver dams have increased local movement, distribution and quality of water. Other species inhabiting the newly created bosque areas include bullfrogs, turtles, trout, pike, catfish, river carp, elk, black bear, cougar, southwestern willow flycatcher, pheasant and grouse. To ensure continued protection of wetland areas, the Tribal Council issued a declaration that 100 feet from the Rio Grande on either side will be forever protected (no development allowed).

Dump Closure and New Transfer Station

It took 2 years for the Ohkay Owingeh to secure funding but only 3 months to complete a project to clean and close a 40-acre solid waste dump. The solid waste collected from the dump site was placed in a small, contained landfill area and capped with 8 inches of topsoil. Native

Former Open Dump Site

Waste Transfer Station

vegetation now covers the landfill, and the former dump is indistinguishable from the surrounding landscape.

To replace the dump, the Ohkay Owingeh installed a waste transfer station, which uses a unique, zigzag design that makes moving bins efficient. To overcome resistance to using the new transfer station, Tribal environmental and sanitation officials held community meetings that focused on the importance of the station in preventing environmental and health hazards, such as solid waste contaminants seeping into well water and groundwater.

Tribal officials are continuing community outreach to encourage station use and compliance. Along with Rio Arriba County, the City of Espanola, and the Pueblo of Santa Clara, the Tribe also co-owns the North Central Solid Waste Authority, which offers a broad range of solid waste services for its customers.

> **"Our goal is maintenance of wetlands by natural means."**
>
> —Charles Lujan, Director,
> Office of Environmental Affairs

Contact: Charles Lujan, Director, Office of Environmental Affairs, Ohkay Owingeh, 505-852-4212 or cwlujan@yahoo.com

Penobscot Indian Nation

The Penobscot Indian Nation of Maine possesses a land base of over 140,000 acres of noncontiguous holdings composed of islands and some mainland parcels throughout the State. The Penobscot holds territory as reservation trust and fee land. Tribal life has always been centered in the Penobscot's traditional homeland in the Penobscot River watershed. Most of the 2,129 Penobscot members reside on Indian Island in the middle of the Penobscot River. Many of the Penobscot's lands are forested, and logging and paper mills are prevalent industrial activities in the area. The Tribal Council is composed of 12 elected members led by a chief and vice-chief.

Painting by Former Chief Barry Dana

The chief of the Penobscot says that their "hands-on," traditional approach has led to environmental and natural resource improvements. The philosophy of a healthy environment inherent in the Penobscot's cultural tradition creates an incentive for Tribal employees to be successful because they know they have a responsibility to preserve the environment for future generations. One member cited the dedication of the environmental staff as an example of the Penobscot's commitment to preserving its surroundings.

Water Quality, Wildlife, and Human Health

The Penobscot Indian Nation has been successful in its efforts to improve water quality, the health of the Penobscot River and related fish and wildlife, and human health. Water quality is a critical issue for the Penobscot because fish and other aquatic life are traditional food sources. Paper mills and other industrial plants discharge dioxins, polychlorinated biphenyls (PCBs), and other wastes into reservation waters. Repeated testing has shown these pollutants have been passed to local fish through the water. Because of this contamination, the Penobscot states that its cancer rate is twice that of anywhere else in Maine.

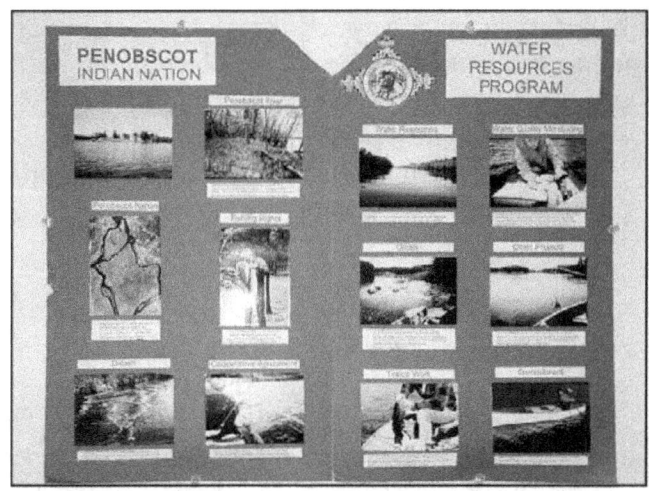

Penobscot Indian Nation Water Resources Program

After much discussion and negotiation, the Penobscot persuaded a paper mill to change its processes to be more progressive and less polluting. The Penobscot thus improved the environment without inhibiting paper mill operations. Quantitatively, the change in mill processes translated to reduced pollution from 10 years ago, and qualitatively, the water looked and smelled better than before.

The Penobscot also has a cooperative agreement with the State of Maine's Department of Environmental Protection to share water quality data and technical assistance. The Penobscot provided water-quality data that supported revised water classifications for more than 500 miles of stream and river segments. As a result, the State of Maine upgraded the protection and classification of these segments for usage and cleanliness. The upgraded classifications provide protections for future traditional uses. The Penobscot also has grant-funded labs to analyze water and air samples and provides water-related education to the local community through school programs, such as "fish friends," and workshops for adults on topics such as non-point source pollution.

Work completed under another Penobscot effort—the Penobscot River Restoration Trust—will result in 100 percent of historical migratory fish habitat on the River being open for the first time in over 200 years. The Penobscot helped to create the Trust under subsection 501(c)(3) of the U.S. Internal Revenue Code to raise funds to restore the River. Participants include American Rivers, Atlantic Salmon Federation, Maine Audubon, the Nature Conservancy, Natural Resources Council of Maine, and Trout Unlimited. To date, two main stem dams in the River Basin are scheduled for demolition to facilitate the transit of Atlantic Salmon, and a fish bypass is planned for a third dam.

The Penobscot has other ongoing efforts to clean and protect local waterways. The Penobscot's contractor invented the "beaver deceiver," a trapezoid structure that protects water outflows to prevent beaver damming. Government agencies rejected the deceiver as a concept that would never work. Penobscot officials continued pursuing the idea, however, until a federal agency awarded grant funding to try the deceiver. The deceiver worked very well and has not only saved the Penobscot about $200,000 in roadwork costs, but also prevented the eradication of many beavers.

Educational Material - "How Mother Bear Taught the Children About Lead"

Lead paint is a problem for the Penobscot Indian Nation, as one-half of all its housing was built before 1978 and is likely to have lead paint. The Penobscot developed the Mother Bear Program to educate its community and highlight the dangers of lead. Mother Bear was based on the Leadbusters Program developed by the State of Connecticut for its schools. According to a Penobscot environmental health official, the *How Mother Bear Taught the Children About Lead* booklet and CD-ROM are effective educational tools. In fact, Tribes from all over the country have asked for Mother Bear Program materials, and 2 years ago, the Penobscot Indian Nation won a national environmental award for the Program.

Educational Booklet

"We have been here for 10,000 years and we plan to be here for another 10,000."

—James Sappier, former Chief, Penobscot Indian Nation

Contacts: John S. Banks, Director, Dept. of Natural Resources, 207-817-7330 or jbanks@penobscotnation.org Dale Mitchell, Environmental Health Tech., 207-827-7401 or dalem@wabanaki.com Penobscot Indian Nation

Native Village of Port Lions

On March 27, 1964, an earthquake and tsunami destroyed the Afognak Village on Afognak Island, a part of the Kodiak Archipelago lying 225 air miles south of Anchorage in the Gulf of Alaska. The Village was home to members of the Alutiiq, who have lived in the Archipelago for about 10,000 years. The inhabitants of Afognak Village relocated to a new site in Settler Cove on nearby Kodiak Island. The new village was named Port Lions in honor of the Lions Club for its support in rebuilding and relocating the village.

Although the Native Village of Port Lions has 425 enrolled members, only about 220 people currently live there. Sixty percent are Alaska Natives. The community of Port Lions is governed by a city government, and the Traditional Tribal Council governs the Tribal organization. Remote and isolated and with no connecting roads to the rest of Kodiak Island, the Village can be reached only by boat or small aircraft, resulting in high transportation costs.

The Village has developed a Comprehensive Community Plan, reflecting its commitment to a "beautiful, healthy, and clean environment" and a "traditional way of life while encouraging progress." Because of the Village's remote location and high transportation costs, a primary concern is waste management. The Tribal Council established an environmental office and an action plan to safeguard public health and involve the community both in developing and achieving community goals, including reducing, reusing, and recycling waste materials. For example, the Village has developed a Solid Waste Management Master Plan, adopted by Port Lions, and formed a Village Environmental Committee, which has developed strong working relationships with the city government and with the Kodiak Island Borough.

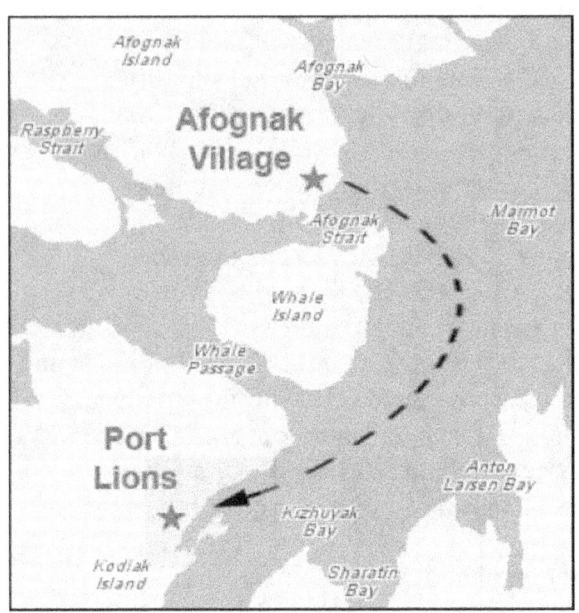

Bear-Proofing the Dump

The 5.73-acre, unfenced dump at Port Lions attracts Kodiak bears, which are found only on the islands of the Kodiak Archipelago. When salmon runs are late or wild berry crops are low, bears depend more on human food and congregate at the dump, strewing trash over large areas. Reaching heights of over 10 feet and weighing as much as 1,500 pounds, the bears can also pose a threat to public safety. The Village is working with the U.S. Fish and Wildlife Service on a bear rehabilitation project to keep bears out of the dump. Currently, the perimeter of the dump is being cleared to facilitate installation of an electric fence. Bear-proof dumpsters will be placed outside the fence.

Clearing Trees for Fence Around Dump

Bear Rehabilitation & Waste Management

Kodiak Bear in the Port Lions Dump

Borough. Success thus far can be measured by the following accomplishments:

- Removing 300 tons of scrap metal.
- Collecting and stocking scrap metal for recycling.
- Cleaning, crushing, palletizing, and shrink-wrapping for shipment and recycling empty 55-gallon drums used for oil, diesel, gasoline, and hydraulic fluid.
- Recycling cans, ink cartridges, batteries, aerosols, fluorescent bulbs, and magazines.

Succeeding at Waste Management

With an emphasis on community caring, trust, and respect, the Village is achieving its waste management goals. Education and outreach programs have successfully promoted responsible hazardous waste practices. For example, Village environmental staff talked to school children about pollutants on Earth Day. They also produced a play "Criteria Pollutants," and children learned about segregating recyclables from hazardous wastes. Educational brochures on recycling, garbage segregation, solid waste management, household hazardous waste, water quality, and indoor and ambient air quality also increased community awareness.

The Village now sends lead acid batteries to Kodiak by Alaska State ferry about twice a year. This effort prevents the 5 tons of batteries that have been recycled to date from leaching into the Port Lions' environment. By making large shipments rather than many small shipments, the Village reduced costs.

In the fall of 2004, Port Lions began recycling through a partnership with the Kodiak Island

In 2005, Village environmental staff gave each Port Lions household a can crusher and a large container to encourage aluminum recycling. The Alaskans for Litter Prevention & Recycling's Flying Cans Program, in association with the Alaska Air Carriers Association, sponsor aluminum recycling. Rural Alaska communities get free backhauling, enabling them to earn money from the sale of cans to the Anchorage Recycling Center. This support is significant, considering the remote locations and high cost of transportation of some native villages.

"We are a small healthy rural community that is a safe place to live where our children enjoy growing, learning and want to stay. We enjoy the peace and challenge of our beautiful, clean environment . . . [and] take pride in our history and cultures. . . . We are a community where families and friendships flourish through caring, trust, and mutual respect."

—Community Vision, Native Village of Port Lions

Contact: Wanda Kaiser, Environmental Specialist, Native Village of Port Lions, 907-454-2234 or wanda@portlions.net

Saint Regis Mohawk Tribe

The Saint Regis Mohawk Tribe is the component of the Akwesasne Mohawk Nation that is located in the United States. The Akwesasne Mohawk Nation also has land in Canada. The Nation's population totals about 15,000 members. The Saint Regis Mohawk Tribe is headquartered in Akwesasne, New York, on about 14,000 acres. Tribal members total about 10,500.

The Saint Regis Mohawk Tribe started its environmental programs in 1978, based on concerns about a large, open dump at a General Motors' plant adjacent to the Tribe and the St. Lawrence River. The Tribe independently learned to put in groundwater wells, collect samples, and monitor and design sampling equipment. It now has its own lab with modern equipment for scheduled testing.

Over time, the Saint Regis Mohawk Tribe has become more sophisticated and is considered a local expert in environmental, natural resource, and human health issues. The Tribe presently has about 30 staff who implement an environmental protection program responsible for air and water quality monitoring, soil analysis, developing and enforcing Tribal standards, sanitation and waste disposal, environmental rehabilitation and reclamation, and emergency preparedness and response.

The Saint Regis Mohawk Tribe promotes an atmosphere of interdependency rather than independence. Tribal officials believe strong external relationships enhance the potential for successful program implementation. Sharing resources with other entities can result in greater efficiency and broader program implementation.

Solid Waste Management

The Tribe established solid waste management services based on input from within the Tribal community. To build interest and reduce resistance, Saint Regis Mohawk officials conducted a community survey in the mid-1990s about Tribal desires for solid waste management. Survey results indicated that Saint Regis Mohawk members did not like outside (non-Tribal) haulers, but would support a Tribally managed solid waste program.

Modular Transfer Station

The Saint Regis Mohawk began curbside collection in 2002 and now has a solid waste management code. The Tribe's residential collection process is "pay as you throw" - $2 per blue bag. The best feature of this system is that users pay only for the amount of trash they generate. The Tribe offers other options for commercial users, such as monthly fees and bulky item pick-up. The Tribe is also working to establish a container service for local businesses.

All waste goes to the Saint Regis Mohawk modular design transfer station. At the transfer station, the Tribe collects both waste and

Waste Management & Educational Outreach

recyclables and processes recyclables for resale. Solid waste services are available to the non-Tribal community as well. Presently, the non-Tribal community uses the Tribe's system on a limited basis. However, Tribal officials hope that, over time, the Tribe's educational outreach program will increase non-Tribal use.

Educational Outreach

The Saint Regis Mohawk Tribe conducts an educational program, "respect, reduce, reuse, recycle," to inform the public about the direct impact of solid waste on the community. The Tribe is also developing strategic partnerships with other entities. For example, the Tribe implemented an agreement with Clarkson University to create a Tribal biodiesel program.

Another outreach activity is a cartoon, *Kwis and Tiio,* on solid waste, energy efficiency, and recycling. EPA granted money to the Tribe in 1997 to develop a solid waste education program that conveyed environmental messages with humor. Two local Mohawk artists created cartoons featuring *Kwis and Tiio* and first published them in 1998. EPA awarded a second grant to continue developing the *Kwis and Tiio* cartoon series, with a focus on recycling and energy efficiency issues. The second set of cartoons was published locally and distributed throughout the United States in the summer of 2000.

Solid Waste Cartoon

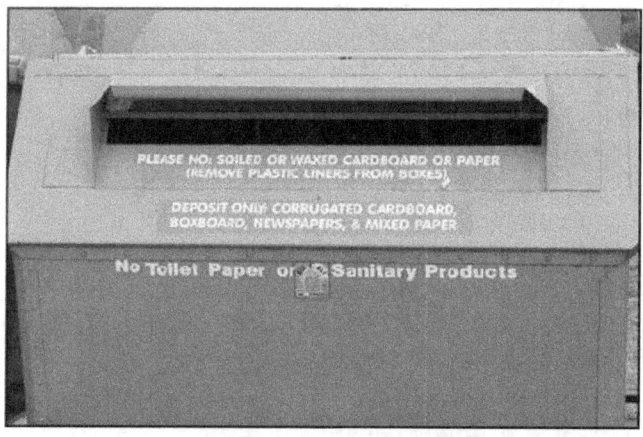

Community Recycling Collection Container

"The Saint Regis Mohawk Tribe is interdependent, not independent from other governments. By working together, you conserve resources and are more efficient."

—James Ransom, Tribal Chief
Saint Regis Mohawk Tribe

Contact: Ken Jock, Director, Environment Division, St. Regis Mohawk, 518-358-5937 ext 116 or ken_jock@srmtenv.org

Sokaogon Chippewa

The Sokaogon Chippewa Community resides on land containing one of the last remaining ancient wild rice beds in the world. Community clans migrated from eastern Canada 1,000 years ago, led by a vision that their journey would end in a land where the "food grows on water," referring to Manomin (wild rice). The annual harvest of wild rice is an important cultural practice for the Sokaogon Chippewa and has changed little in hundreds of years. Wild rice has been an essential resource to Community survival, demonstrated by the Community's willingness to go to war in 1806 to maintain control of the wild rice.

Rice Lake

Today, natural resources are a substantial part of Community culture and are therefore a top priority. The Sokaogon Chippewa consider the most important environmental and natural resource objectives to be protection, assessment, and restoration. The Community emphasizes protection, however, based on the reasoning that successfully protected resources do not need to be part of costly restoration processes.

The Sokaogon Chippewa recently acquired 1,320 acres of land – bringing their total contiguous land base to about 3,250 acres. The Community is relatively small, with about 1,300 members, 40 of whom live on the reservation.

Protecting Water Quality and Dependent Natural Resources

In 2003, the Sokaogon Chippewa Community and the Forest County Potawatomi purchased a mining company and all the land associated with the proposed Crandon Mine for $16.5 million. In early 2006, the Sokaogon Chippewa obtained a bond for $7,948,000 and the Wolf River Protection Fund, Inc. contributed $52,000 to pay off the debt incurred for the purchase. In November 2006, the Sokaogon Chippewa and Forest County Potawatomi obtained all of the mineral rights, timber rights and all other such ties to the former mining land. The pristine water quality essential to wild rice, other wetland and aquatic vegetation, and abundant fisheries is now permanently protected from the threat of the Crandon Mine.

Community opposition to the mine began in 1978, when a mining company submitted permit applications to begin ore mining operations on land less than 2 miles upstream from Sokaogon Chippewa lands. Other large mining companies later submitted permit applications in attempts to gain approval to begin operations. The proposed mine was a major concern for the Community because of the sensitivity of wild rice, fisheries, and other natural resources to changes in water quality. The reservation depends on Rice Lake, a 220-acre wild rice bed that has been the cultural centerpiece of the Community for centuries.

The proposed mine also threatened water quality for other local communities, including the neighboring Menominee, Potawatomi, and Stockbridge-Munsee Tribes. The local communities were concerned about the adverse short- and long-term effects on the environment and natural resources that would result from mining operations. Based on the potential threat to water quality, Sokaogon Chippewa environmental and natural resource officials began

Water Quality & Invasive Species Control

collecting and analyzing water quality data to determine the relationship of water quality to wild rice, fisheries, and other natural resources. Analysis showed that wild rice and other resources are sensitive to contaminants that could result from mining.

To increase awareness of water quality issues associated with mining, the Community conducted an outreach and education program throughout local and state communities. Using modeling and data analysis, the Community presented compelling conclusions about the effect of mining on water quality. With this program, the Sokaogon Chippewa gained needed support throughout Wisconsin, as well as from nationally recognized grassroots organizations. Most important were the relationships built with neighboring Tribes, which resulted in an alliance with the Sokaogon Chippewa and the Menominee, Potawatomi, and Stockbridge-Munsee Tribes. This alliance and other support were extremely effective.

Invasive Species Management

The Sokaogon Chippewa Community has also become involved in efforts to reduce the introduction of invasive species, particularly into water resources, which can adversely affect native vegetation and fisheries. Invasive species that are becoming problematic in the region include the Zebra Mussel, Rusty Crayfish, and various plant species. Of particular concern is the Zebra Mussel, which is showing up in local waters and is easily transferred from one area to another. Lack of public awareness is a primary reason for the undesirable spread of invasive species. To increase awareness,

Wolf River

Sokaogon Chippewa officials conduct an educational and outreach program to inform the community of adverse impacts that can result from invasive species. For example, the Sokaogon Environmental Department conducts a fair each summer to address environmental and natural resource issues and promote effective environmental practices.

During the fair, Sokaogon Chippewa officials use creative approaches, such as games and demonstrations, to educate the community. A great deal of attention is focused on invasive aquatic species. The fair provides an entertaining and interesting approach to teach community members how to avoid the spread of these invasive species.

> **"Common goals, objectives and concerns work for effective relationships regardless of different cultures."**
> —Tina L. Van Zile, Tribal Vice Chair, Sokaogon Chippewa Community

Contact: Tina L. Van Zile, Environmental Director, Sokaogon Chippewa, 715-478-7605 or tinavz30@newnorth.net

Susanville Rancheria

Chartered under the Indian Reorganization Act of 1934, the Susanville Indian Rancheria is located in northeastern California and consists of 427 members of the Maidu, Paiute, Pit River, and Washoe Tribes. The governing body of the Rancheria is the General Council, composed of all the members who are at least 18 years old.

Before 2002, the Rancheria owned just over 300 acres. In March 2002, the Rancheria purchased 875 acres and completed an environmental assessment in 2003. The Rancheria is currently drafting a forest management plan to ensure responsible land management.

In 2003, the Rancheria purchased the 160-acre Cradle Valley Ranch, located near Antelope Lake in Plumas County. For many years, the Ranch had been a private summer home and wilderness retreat. During this time, cattle grazing on the Ranch had eliminated wetland grasses and destroyed Clark's Creek, which runs through the property. The uncontrolled grazing severely degraded habitats for a variety of fish and wildlife resources significant to the Rancheria.

Clark's Creek Prior to Restoration

With funding from EPA, the Rancheria established an Environmental Protection Department, whose mission is to assess, protect, and enhance the environment on Rancheria lands.

The Rancheria's long-term goal is to return Cradle Valley Ranch to pre-settlement conditions. The Rancheria would also like to develop a cultural center and a stewardship area to educate the public about the ways native peoples lived and managed ecosystems. The property will be used for Native American traditional gatherings and ceremonies as well. Currently, no cultural area such as this exists in Plumas or in neighboring Lassen county. The Rancheria included a need for a cultural area in its Master Plan, adopted in 2004.

The first step in returning the property to its pre-settlement condition was to restore and enhance the native ecosystem. Using traditional land management techniques, the Environmental Protection Department accomplished the following:

- Enlisted the help of the U.S. Forest Service to evaluate existing forest health conditions and used the evaluation to guide forest management of the property.

- Partnered with the U.S. Fish and Wildlife Service, EPA, Natural Resources Conservation Service, and North Cal-Neva Resource Conservation & Development to build a fence demonstration project on the Ranch. The purpose of the project, known as the Indigenous Landscape Enhancement Project,

Fencing Demonstration Project

Responsible Land Management

was to keep livestock off the property and allow natural vegetation to recover. The use of barbless wire for the bottom strand of the 2.5-mile fence allowed wildlife, such as deer, safe access to the property.

♦ Developed an Integrated Pest Management program to reduce the spread of noxious weeds on the property.

♦ Consulted with other agencies to restore the water table and natural hydrology of Clark's Creek and improve wetland and fish habitat.

Restored Clark's Creek

♦ Collaborated with a non-profit, the Humboldt Area Foundation, to develop an inventory of traditional use plants and build a garden to propagate native plants for regenerating degraded areas.

♦ Reintroduced traditional use plants, such as elderberry and bear grass, to a 5- to 10-acre area. Rancheria members watered the native plants by hand and fashioned wire cages to protect against wildlife browsing.

♦ Gathered about 500 willow cuttings by hand and planted them along the entire 1/2-mile length of Clark's Creek.

♦ Evaluated photos and collected data to validate efforts that improved fish and wildlife habitat.

Obtaining funding for land acquisition is often difficult for Native American Tribes. The

Rancheria, however, was able to reclaim about one-fourth of the Cradle Valley Ranch purchase price by placing a portion of the property into a 30-year conservation easement under the U.S. Department of Agriculture's Wetland Reserve Program. The easement requires that habitat for wetland, migratory bird, and at-risk species be the primary use of the land. The Rancheria has signed a Wetland Reserve Plan of Operation, which describes allowable land use activities.

Other land management agencies are often unaware of the location or importance of cultural sites on public land. To improve understanding and cooperation in this area, the Environmental Protection Department conducts informal monthly meetings with local representatives from the Bureau of Land Management and the U.S. Forest Service. The Rancheria's Tribal Chairman also meets quarterly with these two agencies.

> **"Treat the earth well! It was not given to you by your parents; it was loaned to you by your children. We do not inherit the earth from our ancestors; we borrow it from our children."**
>
> —— **Ancient Indian Proverb, Susanville Indian Rancheria Master Plan**

Contact: Tim Keesey, Environmental Manager, Susanville Indian Rancheria, 530-251-5623 or tkeesey@sir-nsn.gov

Warm Springs Tribes

The Warm Springs, Wasco, and Northern Paiute Tribes, totaling about 4,400 members, make up the Confederated Tribes of the Warm Springs Reservation of Oregon. The reservation was created by an 1855 Treaty, which ceded 10 million acres of Tribal land to the federal government in return for reserving approximately 640,000 acres in north-central Oregon. The Tribes kept their rights to harvest fish, game and other foods, and pasture livestock in ceded and usual and accustomed lands off the reservation. The Dawes Act of 1887 allowed non-Indians to purchase property within reservation boundaries. The Tribes have repurchased most of that land, however, and today, only about 1 percent of reservation land is non-tribally owned.

The Tribes' economy relies heavily on natural resources, including forest products, hydro-power, and tourism. Tribal management of resources reflects an emphasis on self-sufficiency and on traditional beliefs in unity, spirituality, and respect for the land, water, and each other. In 1992, the Tribes were the first to develop an Integrated Resource Management Plan, which laid out a holistic vision for managing all reservation resources. In partnership with federal agencies, the Tribes also undertook restoration projects in the 8,000 square-mile John Day watershed, which was part of the land ceded to the federal government in 1855. The John Day River is the second longest free-flowing river in the contiguous United States and is the life blood for Native and non-Native Americans.

In October 2002, DOI's Office of Environmental Policy and Compliance awarded the Tribes an Environmental Achievement Award in honor of their "superior accomplishments in environmental stewardship and management."

Integrated Resource Management Plan

The Integrated Resource Management Plan reflects the Tribes' belief that holistic management of resources achieves multiple benefits. The Plan addresses natural resources, such as timber harvests, water quality, and fish and wildlife habitat, as well as cultural resources, such as archaeological sites and traditional plant foods. To incorporate the results of ongoing scientific research in the Plan and keep it in balance with future resource needs, the Tribes review the Plan every 5 years.

Control of 99 percent of the land within reservation boundaries allows the Tribes to enforce Plan policies and practice sustainable forestry. In 2003, Tribal forestry practices were formally recognized and certified as meeting professional forest sustainability standards developed by the Forest Stewardship Council.

Every October, the Tribes host a 3-day harmony workshop for federal agencies to share information about the Tribes and the Plan. The Tribes also host indigenous groups from around the world, including Russia, Brazil, Australia, and Canada, which come to discuss Tribal implementation of the Plan. By comparing present and historic land conditions, the Tribes have made the Plan a dynamic document that reflects changing resource conditions and protects Tribal resources for future generations.

John Day Watershed Restoration

The John Day watershed provides critical habitat for a number of fish and wildlife species, including trout, salmon, sandhill cranes, Canadian geese, and Rocky Mountain elk. Through their John Day Basin Office, established in 1997, the Tribes have successfully partnered with public and private landowners to mitigate damages caused by hydropower production and to help restore the watershed.

Integrated Planning & Watershed Restoration

Since its inception, the Office has completed over 100 restoration projects, including:

♦ Replacing 66 diversion dams that hindered fish passage with fish-friendly diversions to enhance 50 miles of migratory, spawning, and rearing habitat for steelhead and Chinook salmon.

♦ Clearing and replacing 2,387 acres of western juniper with desirable native species to improve headwater flows.

♦ Installing protective fencing and planting hardwoods on 34 miles of riparian land.

♦ Completing seven irrigation projects to increase base flows in the upper basin.

♦ Completing nine underground irrigation pipe projects to cool irrigation water returning to the river.

♦ Installing nine livestock watering areas to divert livestock away from riparian areas and improve riparian habitat.

♦ Establishing a nursery for native plants to provide native cuttings and seedlings for planting in the watershed.

Tree Plantings in a Riparian Area

complete. Federal agencies, on the other hand, are sometimes seen as getting projects started and then moving on, leaving landowners with little support. The Tribes also support local communities by presenting an educational booth at the annual county fair and sponsoring local conservation groups and youth organizations.

Tribal partners include the Natural Resource Conservation Service; Grant Soil and Water Conservation District; Bureau of Reclamation; U.S. Fish and Wildlife Service; Bureau of Land Management; and Bonneville Power Administration, who provided funding.

Fish Friendly Diversion

The Tribes' good neighbor policy has been very successful in creating productive working relationships with ranchers and farmers in the watershed. The Tribes are viewed as a partner that will "stay the course" in achieving restoration goals and be around long after projects are

> **"Decisions and actions may have short-term benefits or consequences, but they also have the potential to impact the environment for several generations. These impacts must be adequately considered to ensure cultural and economic security."**
> — Warm Springs' Integrated Resource Management Plan

Contact: Robert A. (Bobby) Brunoe, General Manager, Branch of Natural Resources, Confederated Tribes of the Warm Springs Reservation of Oregon, 541-553-2015 or rbrunoe@wsTribes.org

Wiyot Tribe

The Humboldt Bay area of northern California is the ancestral home of the Wiyot people, who numbered about 2,000 in 1850. In 1860, settlers massacred Wiyots during their annual World Renewal Ceremony at Tuluwat Village, on what is now known as Indian Island, the center of Wiyot territory. Aside from the Wiyots who were away at the time of the massacre, only one baby, the son of the Wiyot leader, survived. The Tribe's current chairwoman is the great-granddaughter of this lone survivor. By 1910, there were fewer than 100 full-blood Wiyots because of disease, loss of resources, relocation, slavery, and genocide.

The settlers took possession of the 270-acre Island and used it for a shipyard, homesteads, and agricul-

Shipyard on Indian Island

ture. Over time, the Island was contaminated and degraded by creosote and other chemicals used to maintain the ships and by dikes and drains built to control tidal flows. With closure of the shipyard in the 1980s, the Island was covered with dilapidated buildings and tons of scattered metal and wood debris.

An ancient shell mound, comprising 6 acres of oyster and other shells, had been severely degraded, with an estimated 2,000 cubic yards lost between 1913 and 1985. In addition, the shell mound has been heavily looted. As the site of Tribal congregations and feasts over millennia of use, the mound has great cultural significance to the Wiyot people.

Nearly 150 years after the Indian Island massacre, the vision of a restored Indian Island hosting the World Renewal Ceremony is becoming a reality. In 2001, the 500-member Tribe purchased the 1.5-acre shipyard repair facility, the site of most of the contamination and debris on the Island. The ability of the Tribe to

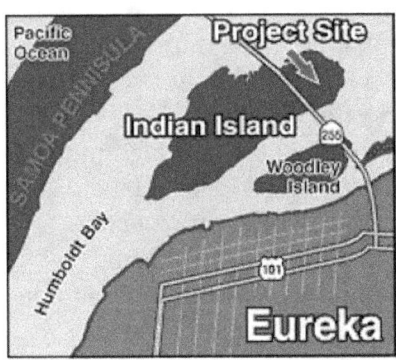

make this purchase was the result, in part, of sunset vigils held since 1992 at the edge of Humboldt Bay in Eureka. Each year, several hundred people gather here, within sight of the Island, to reaffirm the Wiyot dream of reclaiming a sacred site. The vigils have raised community awareness and helped initiate concerted fund-raising efforts, which ranged from selling fry bread and T-shirts to hosting concerts. Establishing the Wiyot Sacred Sites Fund was also a catalyst for fundraising and building partnerships with local organizations.

Restoration began with removing heavy debris from the island. Local organizations stepped forward to help. The Hoopa Tribal Civilian Community Corps and local church groups

helped the Tribe gather tons of metal and wood debris. Because the Tribe did not have a boat, the Coast Seafoods Company offered to transport the debris to the mainland, and Sierra Pacific Industries provided the use of its dock for offloading.

Erosion Control

Restoring Indian Island

A significant challenge was developing a permanent erosion control system. After an extensive research and design process, that included a feasibility study and a geotechnical analysis, the Tribe hired a contractor to install sheet piling along the shell mound and place fill in the eroded area behind the piling. The sheet piling option was chosen for its durability, aesthetics, minimal impact, and affordability. Local oyster growers contributed shells to help stabilize the mound, and the Tribe planted native vegetation to cover the sheet piling. Installation was complete in early 2006. The Tribe will place woody debris collected from the Island to help stabilize the soil and further conceal the sheet piling.

With the success of the Indian Island restoration project, the Eureka City Council voted unanimously in May 2004 to return 60 acres of the Island to the Wiyot Tribe. It was a historic occasion for the Tribe as well as for the City of Eureka, which became one of a small number of cities in the United States to return a sacred site to indigenous people. Currently, the Tribe is using volunteers to remove remaining debris from the Island and has funding in place to:

♦ Construct a dock.
♦ Clean up contaminated soil.
♦ Install a cap on the shell mound.
♦ Restore habitat at the Indian Island rookery, located on part of the Island still owned by the City of Eureka.

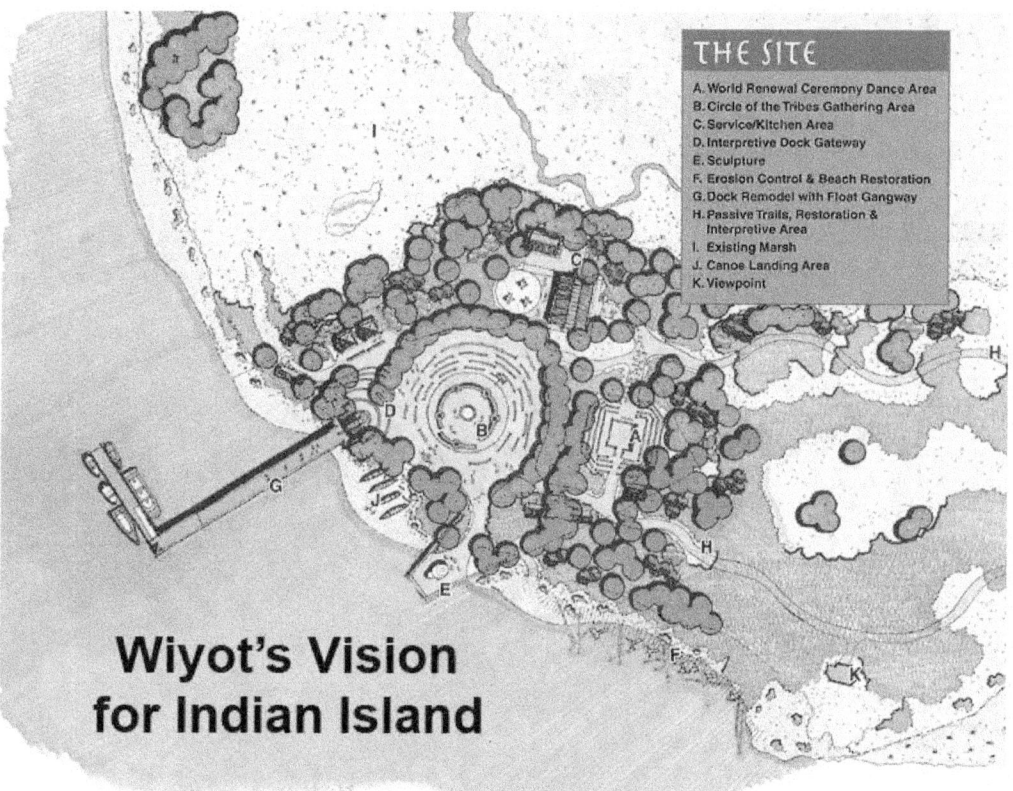

THE SITE

A. World Renewal Ceremony Dance Area
B. Circle of the Tribes Gathering Area
C. Service/Kitchen Area
D. Interpretive Dock Gateway
E. Sculpture
F. Erosion Control & Beach Restoration
G. Dock Remodel with Float Gangway
H. Passive Trails, Restoration & Interpretive Area
I. Existing Marsh
J. Canoe Landing Area
K. Viewpoint

Wiyot's Vision for Indian Island

The Wiyot Tribe's goal is to once again use the Island to host the World Renewal Ceremony on its original location. The Tribe plans to build dance, gathering, and kitchen areas for use in Tribal ceremonies and trails and interpretive areas for the public.

> **"When I'm here, it doesn't make me sad. This is where our family came from.
> It feels good to work here with family and friends, bringing it back. It will happen in my lifetime."**
>
> —Leona Wilkinson,
> Wiyot Council Member

Contact: Jon Mooney, Environmental Director, Wiyot Tribe, 707-733-5055 or jon@wiyot.us

Scope and Methodology

Appendix 1

In December 2005, the EPA Administrator requested that the EPA Inspector General research innovative Tribal practices, with the intention of providing examples of successful environmental programs to other Tribes. DOI's Inspector General agreed to participate in the project to highlight successful natural resource programs and practices implemented by Tribes. The work was performed in accordance with *Government Auditing Standards,* issued by the Comptroller General of the United States. We did not review management controls because they were not related to the scope and objective of our work. We conducted our fieldwork between January 24, 2006 and November 13, 2006 and relied on the Tribes for the accuracy of reported statistics. No prior reports by the Offices of Inspector General for EPA and DOI address the subject matter of this project.

The first phase of the project was to define a successful project and a promising practice. We defined a successful Tribal project or program as a project or program in which positive progress is made towards the environmental or natural resource goals of a Tribe. We defined a promising practice as a Tribal programmatic procedure that we believe provides environmental or natural resource benefit and is transferable among Tribes. Also during this phase, the Delaware Nation volunteered to provide us with examples of its environmental and natural resource programs. We discussed barriers and potential positive practices with EPA and DOI staff and Tribal organization representatives.

The second phase of the project dealt with selecting other Tribes to visit and observe and document innovative practices used as part of environmental and natural resource programs. We developed the selection process to maximize the number of successes and their transferability. We selected the Tribes based on the following criteria:

- Recommendations by EPA and DOI officials.
- Variety of Tribal size.
- Locations distributed throughout the country.
- Variety of program type or focus of program interest (e.g. solid waste management, air pollution control, habitat restoration, recycling, and forestry).
- Willingness of Tribes to participate.
- Review of Single Audit Reports.
- Discussions with EPA and DOI Offices of Investigations.

Each Tribe planned our visits and selected positive practices in their environmental and natural resource programs. During visits, we discussed natural resource and environmental practices; interviewed staff; gathered documentary evidence; inspected, observed, and photographed operations; and analyzed examples of positive practices. Tribes highlighted their success stories according to their individual needs and definitions of success.

This report is not intended to be a comprehensive list of everything federally recognized Tribes are doing to address environmental and natural resource challenges. Rather, the purpose of the report is to focus attention on how some Tribes are addressing environmental and natural resource challenges. The report will provide interested Tribes with examples of successful approaches and points of contact for further discussion and exchange of ideas.

www.ingramcontent.com/pod-product-compliance
Lightning Source LLC
Chambersburg PA
CBHW080631290526
45790CB00007B/3013